ESSENTIAL

INTER

DREAMWEAVER
AN INTRODUCTION

ABOUT THIS BOOK

Dreamweaver: An Introduction is an easy-to-follow guide to
the basic features and the more advanced tools available in
Macromedia's website building program, Dreamweaver 4.

T HIS BOOK IS MAINLY INTENDED FOR
readers with some knowledge of
HTML and the basics of web design
who are eager to explore what an advanced
web design package like Dreamweaver has
to offer. It will help you recognize and use
the main tools and commands in
Dreamweaver. It will describe how to
position elements on the page and format
words, images, tables, and interactive
elements such as forms and JavaScript code.
It will also show you how to build your own
website using the site map function and
upload it to the web using Dreamweaver's
built-in FTP client. While providing an
introduction to the basic features of the
program, this book will also show you how
to explore more advanced features of
Dreamweaver when you feel ready to move
on to advanced web effects.

The chapters and the subsections present
the information using step-by-step

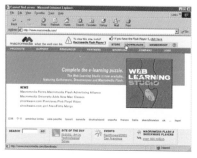

sequences. Virtually every step is
accompanied by an illustration showing
how your screen should look at each stage.

The book contains several features to
help you understand both what is
happening and what you need to do.

Command keys, such as ENTER and
CTRL, are shown in these rectangles:
Enter⏎ and Ctrl, so that there's no
confusion, for example, over whether
you should press that key or type the
letters "ctrl."

Cross-references are shown in the text as
left- or right-hand page icons: ⬅ and ➡.
The page number and the reference are
shown at the foot of the page.

As well as the step-by-step sections, there
are boxes that explain a feature in detail,
and tip boxes that provide alternative
methods. Finally, at the back, you will find
a glossary of common terms and a
comprehensive index.

ESSENTIAL **DK** COMPUTERS

INTERNET

DREAMWEAVER®
AN INTRODUCTION

BRIAN COOPER

**LONDON, NEW YORK, SYDNEY, DELHI,
PARIS, MUNICH, and JOHANNESBURG**

Produced for Dorling Kindersley Limited by
Design Revolution Limited, Queens Park Villa,
30 West Drive, Brighton, East Sussex BN2 2GE
EDITORIAL DIRECTOR Ian Whitelaw
SENIOR DESIGNER Andy Ashdown
PROJECT EDITOR Ian Kearey
DESIGNER Paul Bowler

SENIOR EDITOR Amy Corzine
SENIOR ART EDITOR Sarah Cowley
DTP DESIGNER Julian Dams
PRODUCTION CONTROLLER Michelle Thomas

MANAGING EDITOR Adèle Hayward
SENIOR MANAGING ART EDITOR Nigel Duffield

First published in Great Britain in 2001 by
Dorling Kindersley Limited,
9 Henrietta Street, London WC2E 8PS

2 4 6 8 10 9 7 5 3 1

A CIP catalog record for this book is available from the British Library.

ISBN 0-7513-3359-X

Color reproduced by Colourscan, Singapore
Printed and bound in Italy by Graphicom

For our complete catalog visit
www.dk.com

CONTENTS

DREAMWEAVER BASICS

Macromedia's Dreamweaver is one of the most popular and highly rated web page design and website management programs currently available.

WHAT IS DREAMWEAVER?

Dreamweaver is a powerful web page editing and website management suite that offers both the professional and novice website builder a very wide range of tools and easy-to-apply features for putting ideas efficiently into practice. These features include:

● A WYSIWYG (what you see is what you get) page layout tool

● A site-editing capability (SiteMap) that enables you to add or remove pages without damaging the site's structure. It also contains tools for:

● Adding DHTML (Dynamic HTML) features such as rollover images, animation, and other page elements

● Creating image maps and templates.

● Uploading your completed site by FTP to the web

● Creating and modifying cascading style sheets (css)

● Library items.

WHAT IS A DREAMWEAVER PAGE?

The Dreamweaver interface consists of the document window and a number of optional "floating" palettes. Probably the most important of these is the Property Inspector , which changes its format according to the element (for example, text, image, or table) that is highlighted in the Document window.

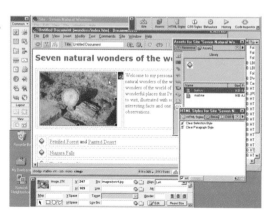

---

17 **Using the Property Inspector**

INSTALLING DREAMWEAVER

If you are not sure whether you need a powerful program of this kind to build your site, Dreamweaver comes in a 30-day trial version: this is a version of the program that simply times out after 30 days. See below for installing this version.

The minimum hardware you need is:
● Intel Pentium processor (or equivalent) 120 MHz (at least)
● At least 32 MB of available RAM
● At least 20 MB of available space on your hard drive.

1 LOCATING THE WEBSITE
● A trial version of Dream-weaver can be found at many major download sites, but we have gone to **www.macromedia.com** in this example. Once there, click on **Downloads**.

2 LOCATING DREAMWEAVER
● Scroll down to the Dreamweaver line under **Macromedia Products** and click the **Try** button.

3 PROCEED WITH DOWNLOAD
● When the Dreamweaver download page opens, click on **Download Trial**.

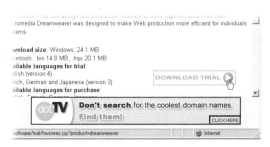

● Click the **Continue Without Login** button.
● You will be asked to fill in information about yourself on a sequence of screens. Complete these and click on **Next**.

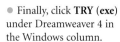
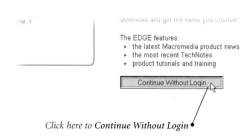

Click here to Continue Without Login

● Finally, click **TRY (exe)** under Dreamweaver 4 in the Windows column.

4 DOWNLOADING THE INSTALLER

● Click in the radio button next to **Save this program to disk** to select it.
● Click the **OK** button.

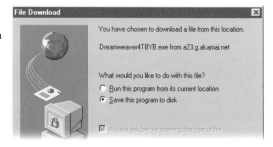

● You will then need to choose a location on your hard disk to which to save the installer file. We have chosen to save to a folder that we have called **My Download Files**.
● Click on **Save**, and the installer will be downloaded to your hard disk.

5 INSTALLING DREAMWEAVER

● To begin installation of Dreamweaver, double-click the installer file. A self-decompression program will now unpack the files required to set up Dream-weaver on your computer.

● When the unpacking is completed, the **Welcome** dialog box will appear. Close any other programs that are currently open, and click **Next**.

● Read the license agreement that appears on-screen, and click on **Yes** to accept the terms of the agreement.

● In the **Location** dialog box, click **Next** (or modify the installation location and then click **Next**).

● Repeat this for the **Start Menu-Program** folder dialog box to determine where Dreamweaver will appear on the **Start** menu.

● Finally, click **Next**.

● The set-up procedure begins. You can follow the progress of the installation in the box that appears.

● When the **InstallShield Wizard Complete** dialog box appears, click **Finish**.

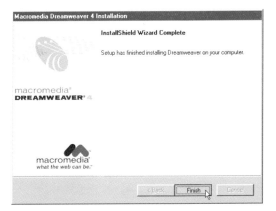

THE DREAMWEAVER WINDOW

This large window is the first that you see when you first launch Dreamweaver. The large area (in which your cursor is flashing) is called the document window. There are several dialog boxes (called "floating palettes") containing various icons, lists, or menus, most of which open more dialog boxes that contain even more options and icons. The next few pages show that easy access to shortcuts and quick launch icons is one of Dreamweaver's most valuable and useful features.

BUTTONS KEY

❶ Object Palette
Click any of these icons to insert that web page element into the page. These elements include image, table, layer, and Java applet (miniature software program).

❷ Document window
This empty window is the virtual page where you design each page to make up your website. When you first launch Dreamweaver, it opens a new document called "Untitled Document (Untitled 1)."

❸ Launcher
Click any of the icons here to open or close the relevant floating palette. You can choose which icons appear.

❹ History
This floating palette contains several palettes. It shows each action carried out, so you can undo or repeat single or multiple actions.

USING THE LAUNCHER

Floating palettes are meant to be a help, not a hindrance, so get used to closing them if they get in the way, and reopening them when you need to open them. Use the Launcher to open or close floating palettes as often as you need them. To close a palette, simply click the relevant icon.

When an icon is depressed, the palette is active. Clicking a depressed icon will close the corresponding palette. Unless you are using a large screen and are seriously multi-tasking, you shouldn't really need to look at the Launcher to see which of the floating palettes are active.

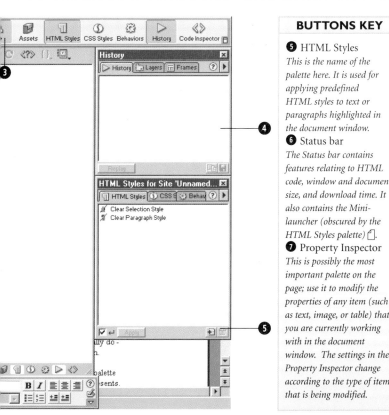

BUTTONS KEY

5 HTML Styles
This is the name of the palette here. It is used for applying predefined HTML styles to text or paragraphs highlighted in the document window.
6 Status bar
The Status bar contains features relating to HTML code, window and document size, and download time. It also contains the Mini-launcher (obscured by the HTML Styles palette) ⌐.
7 Property Inspector
This is possibly the most important palette on the page; use it to modify the properties of any item (such as text, image, or table) that you are currently working with in the document window. The settings in the Property Inspector change according to the type of item that is being modified.

12 Closing palettes

WORKING WITH PALETTES

Before you rush in and begin to create your first web page, it is important to understand and become familiar with the methods used to control the floating palettes and other elements that make up the Dreamweaver interface.

The Launcher does not by any means provide the only method for opening and closing the dialog boxes, as can be seen in the following examples.

CLOSING PALETTES

● In the example here, the Launcher has been used to close the HTML Styles palette. Now that the decks have been cleared in this way, another quick launch option becomes apparent – the Mini-launcher.

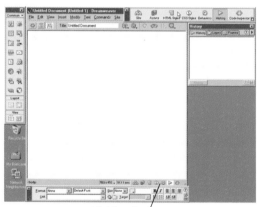

Mini-launcher

● The Mini-launcher on the Status bar is a useful alternative if you need to close the Launcher at any time to free desktop space.

SIMPLIFYING THE OBJECT PALETTE

When starting out with Dreamweaver, it can be difficult to remember what all the icons actually do – despite the fact that a label usually pops up when the mouse cursor is placed over any icon. Use the instructions here to simplify things.

1 SELECTING PREFERENCES

● You can make things a little easier for yourself initially by having the contents of the Object Panel appear as icons and text – at least, until you are thoroughly familiar with what each icon represents. To do this, start by choosing **Preferences** from the **Edit** menu.

2 GETTING ICONS AND TEXT

● Choose **General** in the left-hand panel, click on the down arrow next to **Object Panel** on the right-hand side, and choose **Icons and Text** from the drop-down menu. Then click **OK**.

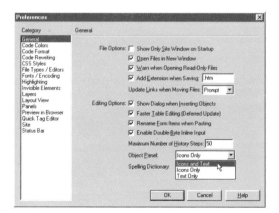

3 VIEWING ICONS AND TEXT

● The floating Object palette contains a brief text description next to each icon.

● To view all the icons and text in the Object palette, click the bottom of the palette and drag down.

Drag the palette down ●

4 ADDITIONAL OBJECT PALETTES

● As well as the Common set of icons, the Object palette contains five further sets of icons.

● To activate any of the other sets of icons, click the arrow immediately below the Object palette title bar and choose the required set from the drop-down list.

● In this example, the "Characters" Object palette has been chosen.

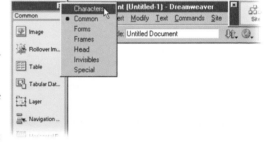

DOCKING AND UNDOCKING PALETTES

The floating palettes enable you to access commands and features quickly and conveniently. You can customize the appearance and composition of these palettes – one of the easiest ways of doing this is by docking and undocking them.

CREATING A SINGLE PALETTE

To undock (remove) the CSS Styles palette from the combined palette to form its own single palette:

● Click the **CSS Styles** tab but do not release the mouse button.

● Keeping the mouse button held down, drag the CSS Styles palette outside the border of the floating palette from which you are undocking it. As you move it, a ghosted frame appears.

● Release the mouse button where you have found a suitable place on-screen to create the new palette. A floating palette called "CSS Styles" appears.

● To dock this floating palette in its original position (or to add it to any other floating palette), repeat the drag-and-drop procedure, releasing the mouse button within the border of an existing floating palette.

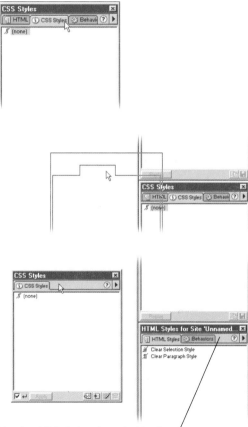

Note that CSS Styles is no longer in this palette ●

CREATING WEB PAGES

Creating simple web pages can be as easy as creating a document using any word processing program. This chapter describes how to build a web page using words and pictures.

INPUTTING TEXT

When you launch Dreamweaver, you begin with the document window on the screen showing a new, blank page ⬜.

It is very unlikely, however, that you will start to create a new web page by typing directly onto the blank page.

METHODS OF ADDING TEXT

To create a web page in Dreamweaver's document window, you can import text from other sources, using the copy-and-paste technique, or you can just start typing on the blank page, as the example here shows. The only formatting used was the inclusion of paragraph breaks. The first paragraph is actually one long line of text that has automatically wrapped to the width of the document window. Paragraph breaks were inserted by pressing the Enter← key. This corresponds to the <p> tag in HTML. To create a line break (equivalent to the <br> tag in HTML), press ⇧Shift and Enter←.

KEYING IN TEXT

● Always use the **Enter** key for items in a list. This example uses the "Untitled" page that opens when you first launch the program. To open a new page at any time, choose **New** from the **File** menu.

● You can format each line, phrase, or word as you go, or type blocks of text and then format them later.

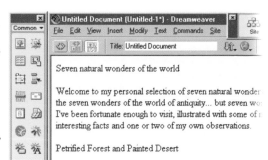

The Dreamweaver Window

10

USING THE PROPERTY INSPECTOR

As we have already seen 🖺, the Property Inspector can be used to format and control text, images, and tables, depending on what is highlighted in the document window at the time. When text has been highlighted, the Property Inspector appears as shown below.

Applying text effects is very simple – just highlight the text you want to change, and then click a button or access a menu from the Property Inspector. For example, you can apply the standard HTML headings and type sizes from two pop-up menus on the Property Inspector.

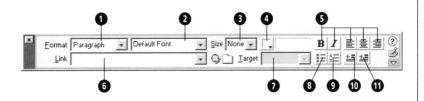

PROPERTY INSPECTOR KEY

1 Format
Use this box/menu to apply a standard HTML heading to text.

2 Default Font
Use this box/menu to choose a specific font or font group for text 🖺.

3 Size
Use this box/menu to apply a standard HTML font size.

4 Text color palette/box
Use this palette/box to apply a color to the text highlighted in the document window 🖺.

5 B/I/next three buttons
These buttons are for applying

formatting effects common to all word processing programs. In order, these buttons will make text Bold, Italic, Left-aligned, Centered, and Right-aligned.

6 Link box/menu
When text is used as a hyperlink, the address of the linked document/item appears in this box.

7 Target box/menu
This box/menu is only used when a hyperlink has been assigned. It determines where the hyperlinked document/item will appear – for example, in a new window or in the frame of a document that uses frames.

8 Unordered list button
Clicking this button produces an unordered list (a list of items beginning with bullet points or other non-numeric symbols) 🖺.

9 Ordered list button
Clicking this button produces an ordered list (a list of list items, each beginning with sequential numbers or letters).

10 Outdent button
Clicking this button will outdent the highlighted text.

11 Indent button
Clicking this button will indent the highlighted text.

6 What is a Dreamweaver page?

20 Adding color

20 Choosing a font

19 Creating Other Text Effects

APPLYING HTML HEADINGS

In HTML, there are six predefined levels of heading, from size 1, the largest, to size 6, the smallest. To create a heading in standard HTML formatting (i.e. Heading sizes 1–6), you need to highlight the text you intend to format.

CREATING HTML TEXT SIZES

● Click the down arrow in the **Property Inspector** on the right-hand side of the **Format** box. Choose the required size of **Heading** from the pop-up list that appears. The highlighted text changes accordingly.

● Using the **Size** box in the Property Inspector enables you to apply HTML size settings that range from size 1 to size 6.

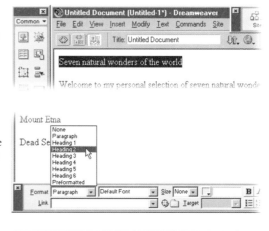

The text size is increased ●

● The default text size for web pages is size 3. You can use the numbers preceded by a + or - sign (e.g. +1, +2) to increase or decrease this default size for any text you have highlighted.

CREATING OTHER TEXT EFFECTS

The Property Inspector can also simplify many other standard HTML formatting tasks – such as turning lines of text into an ordered or unordered list, changing the font, or adding color, or colors, to selected text.

CREATING LISTS

● To create an unordered list, first highlight the lines of text that are to appear in the list, and then click the **unordered list** button in the Property Inspector.

Petrified Forest and Painted Desert

Niagara Falls

The Northern Lights

The Giant's Causeway

Cheddar Caves

Mount Etna

Dead Sea

Click the unordered list button in the Property Inspector ●

● Each list item now begins with a bullet point.

I've been fortunate enough to visit, illustrated with some of my photos, interesting facts and one or two of my own observations.

- Petrified Forest and Painted Desert
- Niagara Falls
- The Northern Lights
- The Giant's Causeway
- Cheddar Caves
- Mount Etna
- Dead Sea

CHOOSING A FONT

● To change the text font, highlight the relevant text in the document window, click the arrow to the right of the **Font** box in the Property Inspector, then choose a font group from the pop-up list. If a visitor's PC does not have the font, the browser moves to the next font in the group.

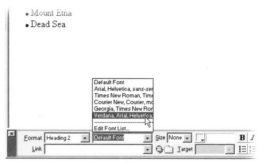

ADDING COLOR

● To add color to text, highlight the text to be colored, then click the button to the left of the **Text Color** box in the Property Inspector. The color palette appears above it, and the cursor becomes a dropper.

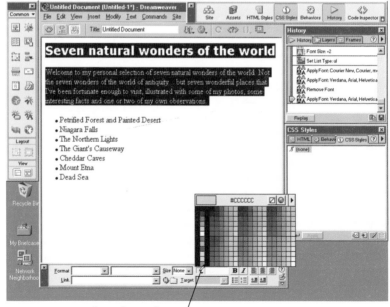

Cursor shows as dropper ●

● Use the dropper to select the color you want to use from the 212 colors available in Dreamweaver (see box below). The new color is now identified (in hexadecimal code) in the color box. At the same time, all the highlighted text in the document window changes to the color you have chosen.

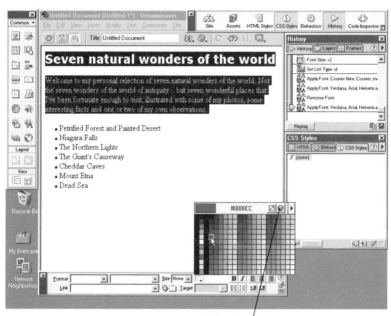

Palette icon ●

PREVIEWING YOUR PAGES

You need to see regularly the results of your web composition and editing. It is good practice to preview your work in as many different web browsers as possible. If you have more than one browser installed, Dreamweaver enables you to preview work in each browser in turn by accessing a single menu command.

PREVIEWING IN THE BROWSER

● To preview the contents of the current document window, choose **Preview in Browser** from the **File** menu, then choose the appropriate browser from the list on the right. That browser will then open, displaying the current document. In this example, only Internet Explorer is available for previewing the web page.

● Note that before you can preview a document, it must first have been saved.

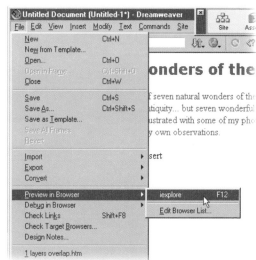

ADDING MORE BROWSERS

● To add more browsers, choose **Preview in Browser** from the **File** menu, and choose **Edit Browser List** from the menu on the right. The **Preferences** window now appears.

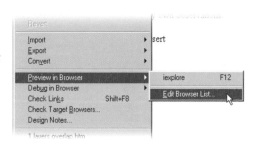

● With **Preview in Browser** highlighted in the **Category** panel, click the + button to the right of **Browsers**. The **Add Browser** dialog box then appears.

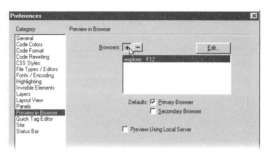

● Click the **Browse** button and the **Select Browser** window appears.

● Navigate to the alternative browser (using the standard method for navigating to/selecting files in Windows 98). Click on the browser's file name to select it, and then click on **Open**. The browser is no longer highlighted in the box above.

● Finally, click **OK** in the **Add Browser** dialog box and then click **OK** in the **Preferences** window.
● New browsers added in this way will now appear in the **Browsers** list when you access **Preview in Browser**.

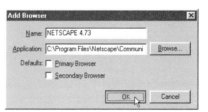

CLOSING THE BROWSER

When you have previewed the current contents of Dreamweaver's document window in a web browser, get into the habit of closing the web browser immediately afterwards. If you leave it open, there is the possibility that you are actually previewing a "temporary" file held in your computer's memory, rather than an accurate preview of the file in the document window. For the same reason, it is necessary to save any work you have done in Dreamweaver before a web browser can accurately preview the contents of the document window.

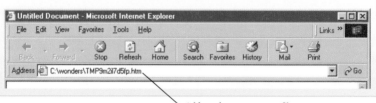

Address shows temporary file

WORKING WITH IMAGES

The following pages show you how to add an image to a web page in the simplest way possible in Dreamweaver. Once you have learned and understood the method, the whole operation can be carried out in just a couple of minutes.

PLACING THE IMAGE

● Place your cursor on the page where you would like the image to appear. (Until you are familiar with advanced image placement techniques, it is best to place the cursor on the left of the page.) Click the **Insert image** button in the Object window.

*Click **Insert image** button*

● In the **Select Image Source** dialog box that appears, navigate to the folder holding the image you want to use, click on it, and click the **Select** button. It is best to work with images that have been stored on your computer.

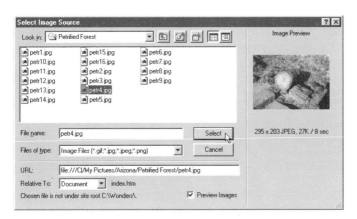

● This automatically saves the image in the same folder as the web page on which it appears. Click **Yes** to continue.

● Click **Save** in the dialog box that appears.

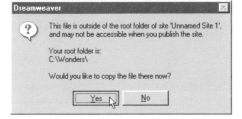

● The image now appears in the document window.

Seven natural wonders of the worl

Welcome to my personal selection of seven natural wonders of the world. Not the seven wonders of the

Image Property Inspector

If you can't see the Property Inspector, open it by choosing **Properties** from the **Window** menu. The "**image key**" box on this page explains the settings that are available for use in the Property Inspector, which will appear as shown here when you have highlighted an image that appears in the document window ⌐.

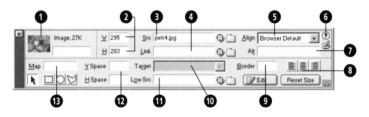

PROPERTY INSPECTOR IMAGE KEY

❶ Image
This shows part of the earlier image and its size in kilobytes.

❷ W/H
These settings in pixels determine the width and height of the image on the page.

❸ Src
Shows the source address for the image. Type the address here, or click the folder icon to the right of the box and navigate to the file's location.

❹ Link
If the image is to be used as a hyperlink, this box shows the location of the page to which the image file is linked.

❺ Align
Clicking the arrow to the right of the Align box provides a pop-up menu containing nine alignment options. Use these to align the image with the text.

❻ Help
Click this symbol to launch the context-sensitive help feature.

❼ Alt
Use this box to type the "alt" text that appears instead of the image in any browser that does not display images.

❽ Alignment boxes
Define the horizontal alignment of the image: left, center, or right. The Align box at the top right specifies the position of the image relative to the text.

❾ Border
The setting specifies the border width in pixels that surrounds the image. The default setting

is 1. To remove the border, type 0 or leave the box blank.

❿ Target
Defines the target of a hyperlink, when the image is used as the hyperlink; locations can be a new window, or a frame within the same main frame.

⓫ Low src
Enables you to use a fast-loading, low-resolution copy of the image, replaced when the final image is fully loaded.

⓬ V space/H space
The vertical and horizontal space in pixels between the image and any other elements.

⓭ Map
Enables you to assign hyperlinks to areas of an image using three area-definition tools.

What is a Dreamweaver page?

ALIGNING THE IMAGE
● Click the arrow to the right of the **Align** box and choose an appropriate setting from the pop-up box. In this example, **Left** was chosen, so that the image has been positioned to the left of the text.

RESIZING THE IMAGE
● To resize the image in the document window, click on the resize handle in the bottom right of the image, hold down the **Shift** key, and drag the cursor diagonally toward the top left.

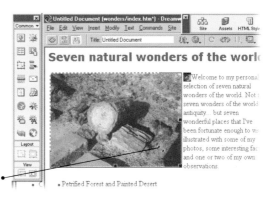

Drag the cursor to resize the image

● The image resizes in proportion. The new dimensions in pixels appear in the W and H boxes in the Property Inspector.

BUILDING A WEBSITE

While the document window is for building individual pages, the Site Map enables you to manage one or more websites simply and conveniently.

CREATING THE SITE

The first stage of building a new site requires you to name your website and create a local root folder. This is the folder on your computer in which all your website folder files are located. It is essential to define this folder when you first set up your site so that Dreamweaver can connect with relative links all the files of your site. A website's home page is almost always located in the local root folder. The home page of any website must be named **index.htm** or **home.htm**, as web browsers automatically load this page first when accessing a website.

NAMING A NEW SITE

● On the document window menu bar, choose **New Site** from the **Site** menu. A Site Definition window appears.

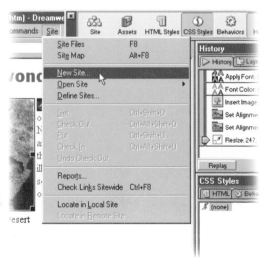

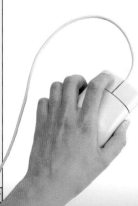

● In the **Site Definition for Unnamed Site 1** box, type the information required into the various fields (see the example below).

● When you have filled in all the relevant entries in the **Site Definition** box, click the **OK** button.

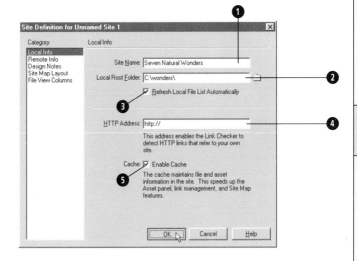

SITE DEFINITION KEY

① Site Name
Type a name for your new website in the Site Name box.

② Local Root Folder
Type a location that forms the local root folder. Alternatively, you can click the folder icon to the right of the address box and navigate to the folder. When you click the Folder icon, the Choose Folder dialog box appears. Navigate to the folder that will hold your website. Click the Select box when you have reached the
appropriate folder.

③ Refresh Local File List Automatically
This box is checked by default. Every time you add, move, or delete a file, the file list within the Local File panel of the Site window will be automatically updated.

④ HTTP Address
This box will contain the web address at which your website will become available to the world. You can safely leave it blank when you first begin to
build a site. The details can be filled in later when you are sure that you have finished experimenting with possible designs and that you are ready to upload the site to a server and go live.

⑤ Cache
Checking this box is highly recommended. Letting Dreamweaver build a cache of all the files you plan to use in your website greatly improves the speed and efficiency of your work.

● If you have checked the
Cache box in the Site
Definition window, a box
tells you that the initial site
cache is being created. If
you try to delete, rename,
or move a file, Dream-
weaver tells you if this may
have an adverse effect.

● All files that you use
when creating a new file
(e.g. image files and sound
files) are now added
automatically to the **Local
Folder** panel of the Site
window. In this example,
the panel shows the web
page and image files created
in the previous example.

ADDING NEW FILES

● To create a new file (web
page) for this new site,
choose **New File** from the
File menu of the Site
window. (Note: the title bar
of the Site window now
shows the name of the site
that you typed earlier in the
Site Name box of the Site
Definition window.) The
file name **untitled.htm**
appears in the Local Folder
window. Overtype this with
the new name. To open this
new file for editing, double-
click its name in the Local
Folder window.

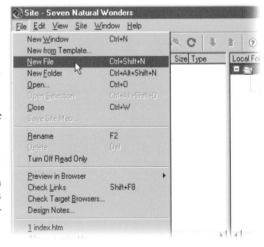

USING THE SITE MAP

The Site Map provides a very useful graphical representation of the structure of a website, enabling you to view the connections between all the files within your site and those on other web pages and FTP sites. It also shows broken connections, enabling you to dive in and troubleshoot.

Using the Site Map also greatly enhances your site management capabilities by making it easy to move files around a site, and to add and delete files without harming the site's structure.

Dreamweaver warns you if any of your actions are likely to break any hyperlinks within the site.

1 VIEWING A MAP

● To view the Site Navigation and Local Folder panels at the same time, click the **Map** icon and choose **Map and Files** from the drop-down menu.

2 VIEWING THE FILES

● If the pages of your website contain no links, only the home page (in this case, **index.htm**) will appear on the map.

● As soon as you create any links ⬀ from (and/or to) this file, the map will begin to take shape.

The example below shows the "Wonders" site at a later stage of development, when links have been

added to the forest.htm, desert.htm, and niagara.htm pages, creating the new map.

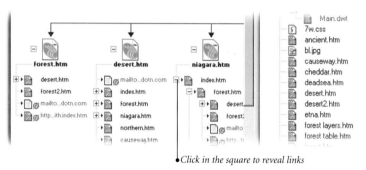

●Click in the square to reveal links

CHANGING THE VIEWING SCALE

● It can be useful to see the Site Map on a smaller scale to get an idea of the overall structure of the site. Click the scale button on the bottom left of the **Site Navigation** panel. Then choose a suitable viewing scale from the options in the pop-up window.

● The Site Map's viewing scale changes accordingly.

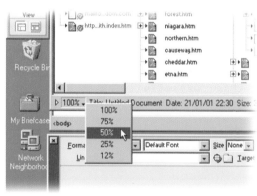

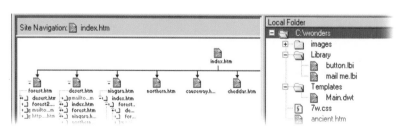

37 Adding Hyperlinks

● You can further adjust the viewing area allocated to the site by choosing **Site Map** only from the **Map** icon in the toolbar, or changing the viewing preferences. To do this, choose **Layout** from the **View** menu.

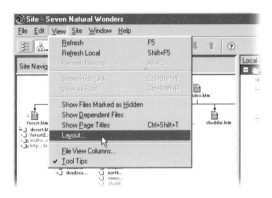

● Change the column width default setting from 200 pixels to a narrower setting (this example uses 80 pixels). Then click **OK**.

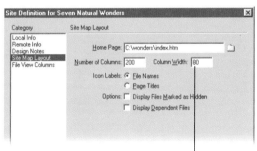

Change default setting ●

● A narrower column width setting, such as the 100 pixels shown here, allows more of the Site Map to be viewed. To find your own preferred setting for viewing, you need to experiment with the column widths.

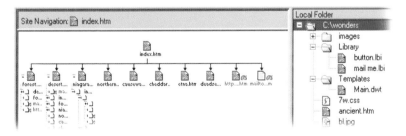

REORGANIZING THE WEBSITE

All aspects of site reorganization can be made simple and safe when you use the Site Map because Dreamweaver always updates all links for you automatically. If you haven't planned for expansion, and you have created all new web pages in the main site folder, it will soon become overcrowded and you will want to reorganize its contents into smaller folders. This example shows how to use the Local Folder panel to move all image files into a subfolder called Images.

1 CREATING A NEW FOLDER

● First, give yourself as much room as possible for the Local Folder panel by clicking the **Site Files** icon that is located in the **Site** window toolbar.

● Click the **Root Folder** (in this example **C:\Wonders**) in the Local Folder panel. (If you intend to create the folder within any other folder, click that folder. In this example, there is only one folder to choose).

● Choose **New Folder** from the File menu. A new folder (called Untitled folder) appears at the bottom of the list in the Local Folder panel.

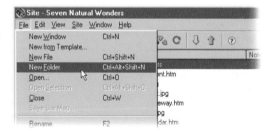

● Overtype this name with the name you require (we have called the folder **images**), and then press the ↵ key.

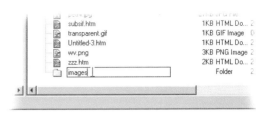

2 MOVING FILES INTO A NEW FOLDER

● Select the files you intend to move into the Images folder (created in the last example) by clicking each file with the Ctrl key held down.

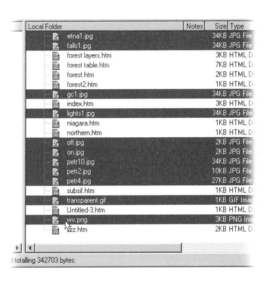

● Keeping the Ctrl key held down, drag the mouse cursor over the Images folder. (This has now automatically moved to near the top of the list in the Folder panel). The **Update Files** dialog box now appears.

● Click **Update** in the
Update Files dialog box if
you are sure that you
intend to move all the files
in the list. If you would like
to reselect the files on the
list or cancel the operation
altogether, click **Don't
Update**, and then repeat
step 2 above. All the files
you selected are now
moved to the folder to
which you dragged them,
and the new site structure
is shown in the Local
Folder panel.

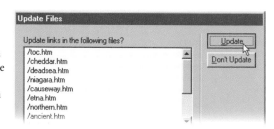

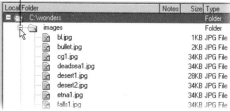

Click here to open or close the folder

PLAN YOUR STRUCTURE IN ADVANCE

Experienced site builders
always give thought to
planning the structure of
the site and anticipating
probable expansion by
creating empty folders for
images, sounds, and applets
in advance. This can be
done either in the site
window, or by creating
folders using Windows
Explorer in the usual way.

DELETE THAT FILE?

If you try to delete a file
that is linked to another,
Dreamweaver warns you
that proceeding may have
consequences for the site's
structure that you weren't
anticipating. If this comes
as news to you, click the
No button and follow the
advice in the dialog box.

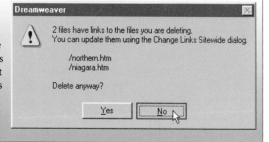

ADDING HYPERLINKS

Hyperlinks are the binding that ties the World Wide Web together. Without links, you don't have a website – just a collection of documents. For this reason, creating hyperlinks is going to be one of the things that you want to do with the most ease in a website design program like Dreamweaver. Fortunately, the procedure is quick and very straightforward. This section looks at the different kinds of hyperlinks that you are likely to want to use on your website.

CREATING A HYPERLINK

You can create a hyperlink from a line of text (or even a single character), from an image (or from a specific area within an image), or from any part of a web page. You can even create a hyperlink from a blank area of the screen, although be warned about following this through, because it might strike visitors to your site as unnecessarily challenging!

LINKING TO OTHER DOCUMENTS ON YOUR SITE

● Highlight the text or image where you intend to provide the hyperlink.

● Click the **folder icon** to the right of the **Link** box 🗋 in the Property Inspector.

17 ❻ **Link box/menu**

● In the **Select File** dialog box, choose the file that you wish to open when the hyperlink is clicked, by clicking once on it. Then click the **Select** button.

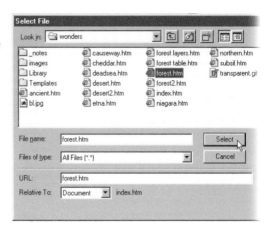

● The relevant text is now underlined in the document window, and the address of the linked file appears in the Link box of the Property Inspector.

LINKING TO WEBSITES

● Highlight the text or image that is to provide the hyperlink. Type the target website's full address (URL), beginning with http://, in the Link box in the Property Inspector. Click on a blank part of the web page. The hyperlink is now complete.

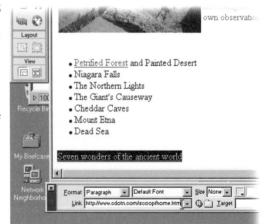

LINKING TO AN EMAIL ADDRESS

● Linking to an email address causes the following to happen. When a visitor to your website clicks an email hyperlink on one of your pages, it causes his/her default email program to open, and the address you have nominated then appears in the **To** field of the email program.

● To create a link to an email address in this way, first highlight the text or image that is to provide the link, and then click the **email icon** in the Object palette.

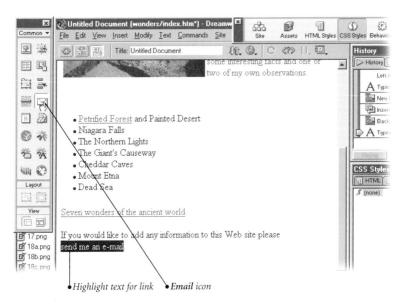

Highlight text for link • *Email icon*

● In the **Insert Email Link** dialog box that appears, type the email address you would like to activate when the link is clicked, and click the **OK** button.

● The email address (preceded by the formula **mailto:**) now appears in the Link box of the Property Inspector.

Address as link •

TABLES AND LAYERS

You can use tables to lay out blocks of tabular data, as in a spreadsheet, but in Dreamweaver you can also use tables to lay out text and images to design entire web pages.

USING TABLES

Creating tables is one of the most frequent things you are likely to do when creating a website. Laying out information, statistics, and lists, and organizing blocks of miscellaneous data on a web page are all much easier and quicker to achieve when you create a table to hold and arrange the data.

CREATING TABLES

● Click the cursor on the page at the point where you want to insert the table. Then click the **Insert Table** button in the Object palette.

Insert Table button

- Petrified Forest and Painted Desert
- Niagara Falls
- The Northern Lights
- The Giant's Causeway

❶ Object palette

● Type the appropriate settings in the Insert Table dialog box. When you have finished typing the settings, click the **OK** button.

● This example and the key below show the functions of the various fields in the dialog box.

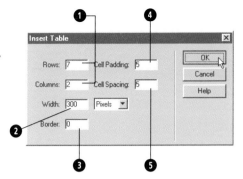

INSERT TABLE DIALOG BOX

❶ Rows/Columns
The number of rows and columns that are to be used in the table.

❷ Width
The table's width can be defined either as a percentage of the browser window width, *or as a fixed width measured in pixels.*

❸ Border
The border width is defined in pixels. Type 0 to omit a border from the table.

❹ Cell padding
This measurement defines the *space in pixels between the contents of the cell and the cell border.*

❺ Cell spacing
This defines the space between individual cells, with the cell spacing measured in pixels.

● The table outline now appears on the page. The Property Inspector changes to the appropriate format for tables, containing the settings you chose in the Insert Table dialog box.

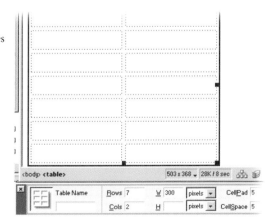

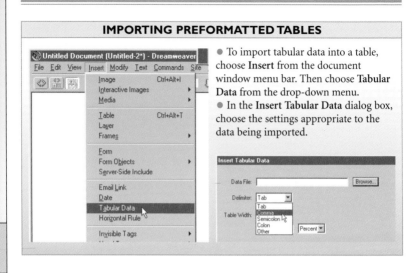

IMPORTING PREFORMATTED TABLES

● To import tabular data into a table, choose **Insert** from the document window menu bar. Then choose **Tabular Data** from the drop-down menu.

● In the **Insert Tabular Data** dialog box, choose the settings appropriate to the data being imported.

INPUTTING DATA

After you have created a table, you can type the data straight into the table or copy and paste it from another source.

This can be from another part of the document, the clipboard, or from any other document open on your desktop.

MOVING DATA

● If the data you want to include in the table appears in another position on the same page as the table, you can highlight it and then drag-and-drop it into the table field, as shown in this example.

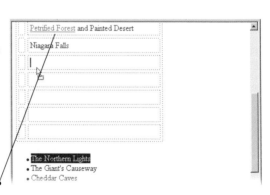

Position for highlighted text ●

CHANGING COLUMN WIDTH

● To change the width of the columns, move the cursor over the column divider. The cursor now changes shape. Click the mouse button, keep it held down and drag the column divider to the left or right as required.

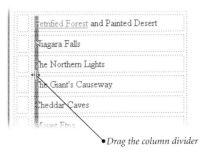

● *Drag the column divider*

● You can also use this method to create sophisticated bullet effects. To do this, create a two-column table and use a graphic in the left-hand column and the hyperlinked text entry in the right-hand column.

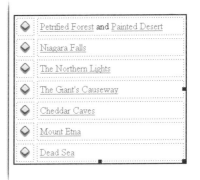

● When you view this table in the web browser, the table grid disappears and you are left with the bullet and hyperlinked text effect. When we first set up this grid, we did so with 0 as the (invisible) border setting ▯.

40 **Creating tables**

USING TABLES FOR LAYOUT

Tables aren't just useful tools for laying out tabular data. They are also widely used for laying out pages.

Page layout for web browsers using the most basic HTML tags is far from being a precise science. What may look good on your web browser on your computer may look very different on someone else's computer. Web pages don't necessarily work like the printed page. When a visitor to your website opens one of your web pages, there are many factors that could make your carefully planned layout flow into unexpected areas of the browser page.

WRAPPING AND REFLOWING TEXT

● The first example here shows Microsoft Internet Explorer wrapping the text around the image when the browser is set at a certain width. (In this example, the bulleted text has not been put in a table.)

● When the browser is at the same width using Netscape Navigator, however, the text does not wrap. It all appears to the right of the image.

GETTING RID OF REFLOWS

Using tables to lay out parts or all of your web pages provides a simple solution to this problem of text reflowing.

● One way of getting around all this is to use tables to set the width of a page or elements within a page. So, you could create a table 600 pixels wide, and place rows, columns, and cells within that to hold paragraphs of text, images, and so on. This gives you much more control over the design of your page, and prevents the text and images reflowing when the browser window is resized.

The example shown below uses a 600-pixel-wide, two-column table to contain the image and text at the top of this page.

Seven natural wonders of the world

Welcome to my personal selection of seven natural wonders of the world. Not the seven wonders of the world of antiquity... but seven wonderful places that I've been fortunate enough to visit, illustrated with some of my photos, some interesting facts and one or two of my own observations.

◇ Petrified Forest and Painted Desert

● Note that now, when viewed in the browser, the text no longer wraps to fit the page. The image and text both remain at a fixed width, defined by the table. The list below is contained within a second table of fixed width (300 pixels).

CREATING NEW COLUMNS AND ROWS

The following example describes how to use Dreamweaver to create one or more columns in a table, but this procedure is equally applicable to creating rows (by substituting Row for Column in each of the steps shown below).

INSERTING COLUMNS
To create one or more columns on the right-hand side of a table:

● Place the cursor inside one of the cells in the column farthest to the right within the table.

● Right-click the mouse and choose **Table**, and then **Insert Rows or Columns** from the drop-down menu.

● In the **Insert Rows or Columns** dialog box, click the **Columns** button.

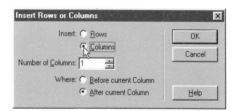

● In the **Number of Columns** box, type the appropriate number of columns to be inserted in the table. Click the appropriate button (**After current column**, in this example) next to Where.
● Finally, click **OK**.

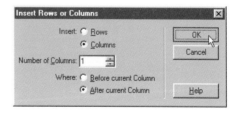

● A new single column now appears, inserted after the current column.

● Clearly, this method can be used to insert rows or columns before or after the position in which the cursor has been placed.

The new column appears to the right of the existing two columns, within the space allocated to the table

USING LAYERS

Layers are containers into which you can load text, images, objects such as Java applets, and even other layers. You can then drag them around the document window until you get exactly the design you want. Layers can produce very sophisticated effects, including the use of visible/invisible layers and animation.

The designer needs to make a decision about whether to exclude certain readers from the pages, because web pages that use layers only work properly in version 4 or higher of Microsoft Internet Explorer and Netscape Navigator.

CREATING LAYERS

● Place the insertion point in the document window where you want to insert the layer. Then click the **Insert Layer** button on the Object palette.

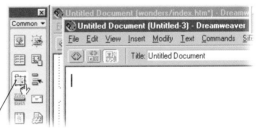

Insert Layer button

● You will observe that the mouse cursor now changes to a cross-hair.

● Hold down the mouse button and drag the cursor diagonally downward, releasing it when the box is the appropriate size. You can easily return and alter the dimensions of the box at a later time if necessary, so you can afford to use approximate sizes when you first create a layer.

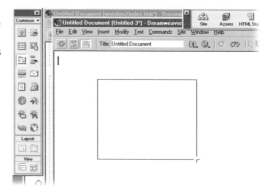

INSERTING TEXT

● To insert text inside a layer, place the insertion point inside the layer box and click the mouse button.

Insertion point created ●

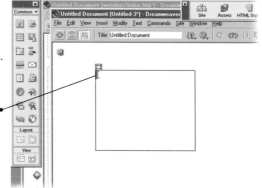

● You can then start typing. The text can be formatted in the usual way using the Property Inspector 🗋. This reverts to its text format while you are in text-handling mode.

MOVING LAYERS

● To move a layer, click on its border. When you move the cursor over the border of the layer, the cursor changes to a heavy cross-hair. When you click on the border, the cursor changes shape again.

● To move the layer, keep the mouse button held down, and drag the whole box, releasing the mouse button when it is in the appropriate position on-screen. As you move the layer, the cursor changes its shape, and the ghosted outline of the box remains in its original position.

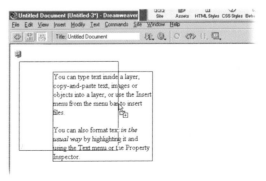

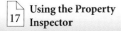

Using the Property Inspector

17

● When you release the mouse button, the layer is set in its new position on the page.

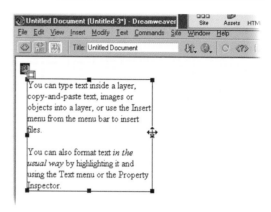

● Note also that whenever you select a layer by clicking on its border, the Property Inspector changes to the format appropriate for layers.

RESIZING LAYERS
● To resize a layer, click one of the points on the frame and move it in the appropriate direction. For example, to increase the height of a layer, click the point at the bottom of the layer in the middle, and drag the cursor downward, releasing the mouse button when the appropriate size is reached.

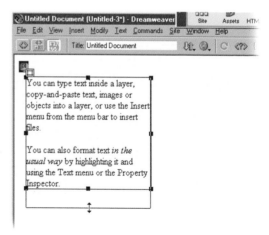

● To resize the whole layer, click one of the corners and drag diagonally in the appropriate direction. (In this example, the layer is being expanded.)

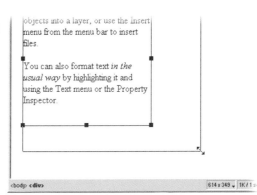

● When you have expanded the layer to the required width and height, release the mouse button. The text will expand to fill the width of the newly expanded layer.

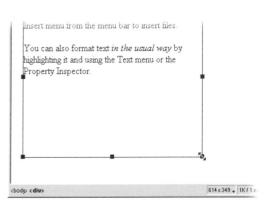

LAYERS TO TABLES

Web browsers earlier than version 4 of Netscape Navigator or Internet Explorer will have difficulty in displaying web pages that rely exclusively on layers. For this reason, web page designers often convert layers to tables before making their finished websites available. Please note that you cannot convert overlapping layers into tables, so bear this in mind when planning.

TIME SAVERS

Creating and using templates, and adding library items, can save you a great deal of time when you are adding new pages or sections to your website.

USING TEMPLATES

Templates can save a lot of time, and are ideal for giving your website a consistent look. This may be created by the site-wide use of a color scheme, for example, or by using design components in exactly the same positions on each page.

SETTING UP A TEMPLATE

When creating a new template, you clearly want to consider using elements that are known to work across a range of pages or the whole site. In this example, we are adding a navigation bar at the bottom of the window, but logos and recurring links (perhaps to your email and/or postal address) are also popular standard elements used for templates.

1 CREATING A WEB PAGE

● To begin, create a web page using the methods described in the previous sections of this book. The example here shows a simple table that has been divided into five main cells. The cell at the bottom has been further divided into nine cells, each of which contains the main pages or sections of the website.

2 CREATING HYPERLINKS

● Create links in the usual way for each hyperlink – highlight the text that is to be the hyperlink, then click the **folder icon** next to Link in the Property Inspector. Navigate to the appropriate page and click **Select** in the **Select File** box)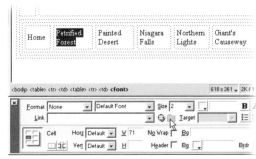

3 SAVING YOUR WORK

● The first time you save your work, choose **Save As Template** from the **File** menu. (Subsequently, choose **Save** from the File menu as usual.)

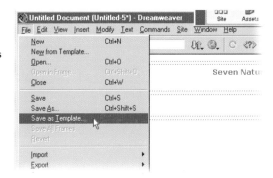

4 NAMING THE SAVED WORK

● The **Save As Template** dialog box appears. The site in which you are currently working will appear in the Site box. In the **Save As** box, overtype the **Untitled** name that appears by default with the name you wish to give the template. Then click **Save**.

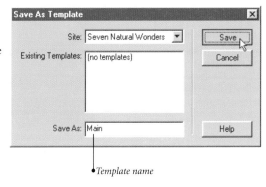

●*Template name*

5 CHECKING THE SAVED FILE

● The word **Template** now appears in the title bar of the document window, followed by the name you have given to the template.

● When you next look in the Templates folder of your website, the file will have a **.dwt** extension.

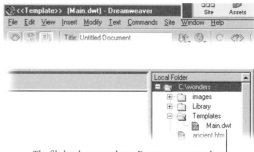

The file has been saved as a Dreamweaver template ●

EDITING THE TEMPLATE

Before you can use a template to create new documents, you must assign certain areas of the template as editable, or else you won't be able to add anything at all to the page. The whole point of a template is that certain areas remain fixed. These areas are, in the following example, the navigation bar at the bottom of the page, the site name at the top right of the page, and the margin on the left of the page. The rest of the page (the areas that are not highlighted) will be editable.

1 CREATING EDITABLE REGIONS

● In the template you have just created, right-click on the area of the page that you wish to designate as editable, and right-click the mouse. Now choose **New Editable Regions** from the pop-up menu that appears.

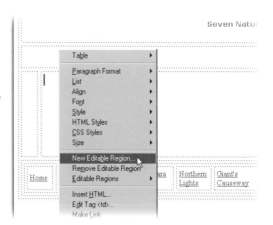

2 IDENTIFYING THE REGION

● In the **New Editable Region** dialog box that appears, type a name to identify that editable region in the **Name** box (**Body** in this example), and then click the **OK** button.

● That word now appears in curly brackets, and is highlighted in color on the appropriate part of the template page.

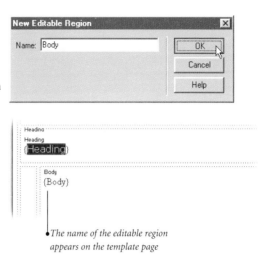

● *The name of the editable region appears on the template page*

● It is up to you to format the text in the editable regions of a template. When you open a new document based on that template, the positioning, font, and other aspects of the formatting are retained.

● In this example, the **Heading** editable region has been formatted so that any text typed within it will automatically be Verdana/Arial/Helvetica, Heading 3 size, color #000066.

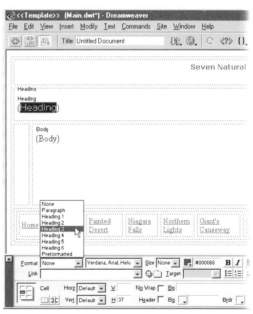

● The formatting decisions that you have made for the **Heading** region are visible when you open a new document based on this template.

3 REPEAT THE PROCEDURE

● If you try to save a template without first creating editable regions, this warning box appears. If this happens, click **Cancel** and create the required editable regions.

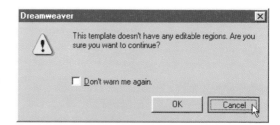

● To open an existing template for editing, go to the Site window and double-click the **Templates** folder icon to open it. Then double-click the appropriate template file name. The template will now be open for editing.

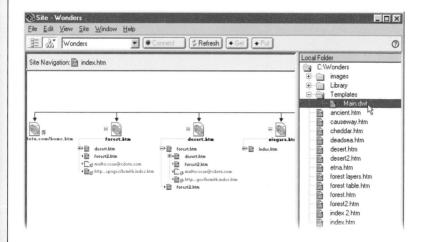

OPENING A NEW DOCUMENT
FROM A TEMPLATE

When you open a new document based on a template, you have the advantage of finding all the common elements in place.

In addition, when the new document is edited, all pages based on it are automatically updated.

1 SELECT A TEMPLATE

● Choose **New from Template** from the File menu. The **Select Template** dialog box appears.

● First, ensure that the correct site is chosen in the Site box. Then click on the required template in the Templates box. (In this example, there is only one template available.)

2 WORKING ON THE NEW PAGE

● The new page appears, based on the template you have chosen. You will see the name of the template in the top right corner of the page. The beginning of each editable region is indicated in small type against a blue background.

● You can overtype or delete the words **Body** and **Heading** that appear within the curly brackets.

ADDING ITEMS TO THE LIBRARY

The library enables you to group together useful items that you can add to or draw from at any time when creating web pages.

The library can contain virtually anything that you can highlight and drag into the library window.

1 OPENING THE LIBRARY

● Click on the **Assets** button on the Launchpad. The Library palette appears.
● Click the **Library** button.

Library button

2 SELECTING THE LIBRARY ITEM

● Highlight the material that you would like to make into a library item; then drag it into the Library palette and release the mouse button.

Highlighted material

3 CREATING A TITLE

● An icon now appears, with the word **Untitled** highlighted in the adjacent text box. Overtype this with a descriptive word or phrase by which you can identify the library item (in this case, **mail me**).

4 CHECKING THE LIBRARY ITEM

● When you next click off the material that you highlighted in the document window, it appears as highlighted text. This indicates that this material is a library item and cannot be altered unless you either edit or detach the material from the library ⌐.

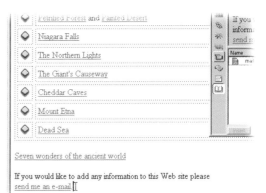

ADDING UNDRAGGABLE ITEMS

There will be times when you have difficulty dragging items into the library palette (perhaps because they are too small to select easily). This problem can be overcome by using the following options in the document window menus.

1 ADDING AN ITEM TO THE LIBRARY

● Click on the item to be made into a library item. Then click on the **Modify** menu. Choose **Library** and **Add Object to Library**.

Chosen item

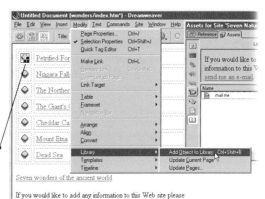

⌐ Creating a
63 Customized Style

2 SELECTING AND TITLING

● Then it is easy to follow steps 3 and 4 on page 58 to name and check the new library item.

USING LIBRARY ITEMS

Adding a library item to a page is a simple drag-and-drop procedure that involves locating the item in the library palette and then placing it in the required position on the page. It is a similar process to creating a library item, only this time in reverse.

1 LOCATING THE ITEM

● To add a library item, drag an item from the Library palette to the desired point in the Document window. The importance of naming library items clearly and descriptively becomes increasingly apparent as you begin to accumulate a long list of items in the Library palette.

58 **Adding Items to the Library**

2 POSITIONING THE ITEM

● Release the mouse button at the point on the page where you intend the library item to appear. The item now appears within a highlight when you next click elsewhere on the page.

EDITING LIBRARY ITEMS

It is not possible to edit a library item when you have placed it on the page. If you want to change an instance of a library item on a page, you need to delete it and retype it (or redesign it), or detach it from the library.

1 OPENING THE ITEM

● To open a library item for editing, right-click the item on the page where it appears and choose **Open Library Item** from the drop-down menu. (Alternatively, click on the item, and then click the **Open** button in the Property Inspector.)

2 EDITING THE ITEM

● Edit the library item as required. (In this example, the library item comprises one line of text. A few words have been deleted from the beginning of the line.)

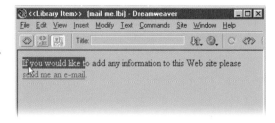

3 SAVING THE CHANGES

● Next, save the changes by choosing **Save** from the File menu. Finally, close the window for that library item.

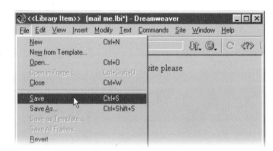

● If the library item appears on other pages in your website, these appear in the **Update Library Items** dialog box. Click **Update** to update all occurrences. Then click **Close** in the next dialog box to complete the process.

● The example here, and every other instance of the library item on the website, is now changed accordingly.

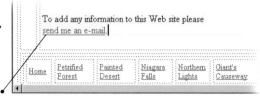

The amended text is highlighted

CREATING A CUSTOMIZED STYLE

A style in Dreamweaver is a list of customizable rules that can be applied to text and other HTML elements in a web page. It enables you to name and define new styles, or adapt existing HTML definitions, and apply them to one or more web pages, or across an entire site. For example, you could create a style based on 14pt, bold, italicized, blue, underlined text and call it **myText**.

Subsequently, every time you apply the **myText** style to any text, the text becomes linked to that style. If you later decide to change the definition of the style, the linked text is automatically changed as well.

USING STYLES

If they are utilized correctly, an author can use styles and style sheets to effect changes rapidly within a web page or across a whole site. This procedure uses methods that are very similar to those described earlier for creating and working with templates and library items.

1 CREATING A NEW STYLE

To create a new style, do the following:

● Click the **CSS Styles** button in the Launchpad, and the CSS Styles palette now opens.

● Click the **New Style** button at the bottom of the CSS Styles palette.

Click the CSS Styles button

Click the New Style button

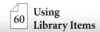

2 SELECTING A NAME

● Click the **Make Custom Style (class)** radio button. Then type a name in the Name box (**.mainHeading** in this example) and click **OK**. The Define In dialog box appears. Choose a name for the style sheet and location to save it in, then click **Save**.

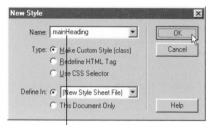

● *All custom style names begin with a period – if you forget to type it here, Dreamweaver automatically adds it for you*

3 CHOOSING SETTINGS

● With **Type** highlighted in the **Category** panel on the left, choose any settings you require from the drop-down menus and check-boxes on the right. When you have chosen, click the **OK** button.

● In the **Save Style Sheet File As** box that appears, choose a name and location for the file, and click **Save**.

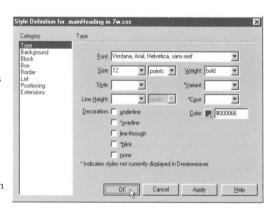

USING CSS

CSS, or Cascading Style Sheets Level 1 (CSS-1), to give style sheets their full name, provide authors with a means for expanding the capabilities of HTML by enabling them to apply color, type face, size, and other formatting to text. Styles can have much wider applications regarding the redefinition of HTML tags. For example, one very common use of CSS is to remove the underline from links on web pages.

With all this, however, an important drawback of CSS-1 is that it only operates properly in version 4 or higher of the main web browsers, Microsoft Internet Explorer and Netscape Navigator. Even in such versions, there are still some anomalies between the application of styles in these browsers.

4 APPLYING THE STYLE

● The CSS Styles dialog box now contains the style that you have just created. In order to apply this particular style to any text, highlight the text in the document window, and then click the style's name located in the CSS Styles dialog box.

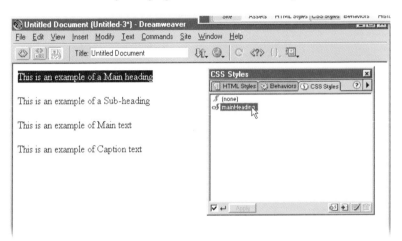

● Follow the same procedure to add more styles to your document.

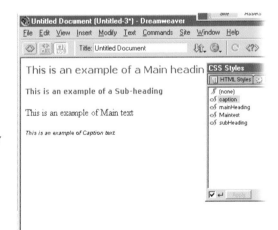

Editing styles
To edit CSS styles at any time, open a web page that uses the styles. Then open the **CSS Styles** dialog box, double-click the style you wish to edit, and finally make the required changes.

PUBLISHING A WEBSITE

Once you have finished building your site on your computer, and have thoroughly tested the validity of all the links, it is time to take the plunge and unveil it to the viewing public.

DREAMWEAVER AND FTP

The usual way for a home user to publish a website is to create the site at home and then copy it to a server owned by the Internet Service Provider (ISP), from which it becomes accessible. How you do this depends largely on the arrangements made with your Internet Service Provider. This section shows how to publish a typical non-business-user's site, but the principles are the same for most types of site. When this site has been completed, the next stage is to transfer it to the File Transfer Protocol (FTP) site. FTP provides the method by which files are transferred between computers and servers. (Copying files from your computer to the server is uploading. Copying files from the server to your computer is downloading.)

USING FTP

Dreamweaver has a built-in File Transfer Protocol capability that enables you to drag-and-drop files between your computer and your ISP's server. To use this feature, you need to provide some Site Definition settings that are based on information provided by your ISP.

SETTING UP AN FTP SITE

● From the main Dreamweaver window, choose **Define Sites** from the Site menu. The Define Sites dialog box appears.
● Choose the appropriate site name and click the **Edit** button. The Site Definition dialog box appears.

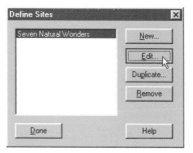

● Click **Remote Info** in the **Category** panel on the left of the Site Definition dialog box, and choose **FTP** from the drop-down menu next to **Access**.

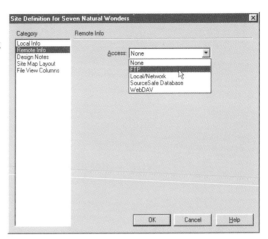

● Type the FTP details required for posting your website into the appropriate boxes. Then click **OK**. The example below shows some typical settings.

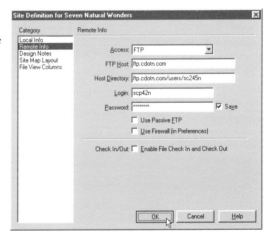

● Next, you are returned to the Define Sites dialog box. Click **Done** to complete the procedure.

UPLOADING AND DOWNLOADING FILES

When the FTP settings are in place, you can begin moving files backward and forward between your computer and the FTP site that hosts your website. Dreamweaver maintains parallel file and folder structures between your local site (the files on your computer) and the remote site (the files on the server). In addition, Dreamweaver warns you if you are about to overwrite or delete any files that may have a harmful effect on the integrity of your website – make sure you read these messages carefully before clicking any **OK** buttons.

UPLOADING YOUR FILES

● To upload to the FTP site, connect to the internet, then click the **Connect** button at the top of the Site window. A **Connecting to...** box appears, informing you of the connection status to the FTP server.

● Now choose **Site Files** from the Window menu.

● When you are connected to the FTP server for the first time, the contents of your website appear in the right-hand window (under Local Folder), and as an empty window on the left (under Remote Site).

● To copy your website to the FTP site, click the **top-level folder** in the right-hand window, drag it over the left-hand window, and release the mouse button.

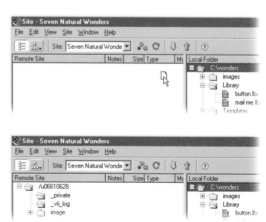

● When you have finished copying files between the server and your computer, close the connection by clicking the **Disconnect** button at the top of the Site window.

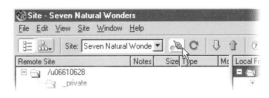

● To look at your site live on the web, type its web address in the address box of your web browser. To copy a file from the server, follow the same procedure, but this time drag the files from the left-hand window to the right. (The path settings typed into the FTP settings box earlier ensure that the Site window displays appropriate local and remote sites when you connect to the FTP server.)

COPYING DEPENDENT FILES

● The main exception to the rule involves dependent files. If you try to copy a file that contains links to other files on your site, which must also be copied for the site to work correctly, the **Dependent Files** prompt box appears. In nearly all cases, click the **Yes** button.

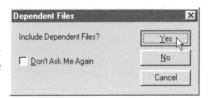

KEEPING THE NEWEST FILES

● Dreamweaver warns you when you are about to overwrite files on the server with older versions from the local folder on your hard disk. If you see a dialog box like this one, click **No** to all and then check very carefully whether you really intend to upload an older version.

GLOSSARY

CACHE
In Dreamweaver, a folder that holds a record of existing files in a website to enable links to be updated quickly when any file is moved, renamed, or deleted.

CSS
Cascading style sheets. These enable authors to apply type face, size, color, and other formatting to text.

DOWNLOAD
The process of transferring a file from a remote computer to your computer.

FREEWARE
Software that can be freely used and distributed, but the author retains copyright.

FTP
File Transfer Protocol. The usual method used for copying files between the local site (on your computer) and the remote server to update your website.

GIF
Graphics Interchange Format. A compressed image format limited to 256 colors, ideally suited to images with large areas of flat color, such as buttons and similar web graphics.

HOME PAGE
The main page of a website, usually called home.htm or index.htm. This page is opened first when you visit a website.

HTML
Hypertext mark-up language. The "tagged" formatting language in which web pages are written.

HYPERLINKS
Part of a web page (text, image, table, etc.) that links to another document or file on the internet.

HYPERTEXT
Text that links to other parts of a document, or to documents held on another computer. Clicking a hypertext link takes you to the linked document.

ISP
Internet Service Provider. Any organization that provides access to the internet.

JAVASCRIPT
Script language that enhances the interactivity of web pages.

JPEG (JPG)
Joint Photographic Experts Group. One of the most commonly used image formats on the internet. Its highly compressed image format means that it is widely used for photographs.

LAYER
A container in Dreamweaver into which text, images, objects, and other layers can be loaded.

NETWORK
A group of interconnected computers that exchange data.

PATH
The address of a file on a computer system.

PIXEL
A unit of measurement for computer displays. A display consists of a series of pixels that display images on screen.

PNG
A widely used compressed image format on the web that, like the JPEG format, can display millions of colors.

PROPERTY INSPECTOR
A Dreamweaver palette that enables the user to define the properties of any item (text, image, table, layer, etc).

ROLLOVER
In web pages, the swapping of one image for another when the mouse cursor passes over, giving the effect of animation.

SERVER
Any computer that allows users to connect to it and share information and resources held on it. The term also refers to the software that makes the information available for downloading.

SHAREWARE
Software that is made freely available for use on a try-before-you-buy basis.

STATUS BAR
The area along the bottom of the web browser window that shows a URL when the mouse cursor points to the hyperlink. (The status bar can also be used to display text messages defined using JavaScript code).

UPLOAD
The process of transferring a file from your computer to a remote computer.

URL
Universal Resource Locator. An address on the internet.

INDEX

ACKNOWLEDGMENTS

PUBLISHER'S ACKNOWLEDGMENTS
Dorling Kindersley would like to thank the following:
Paul Mattock of APM, Brighton, for commissioned photography.
Microsoft Corporation for permission to reproduce screens
from within Microsoft® Windows® 98.

Screen shots of Dreamweaver® 4 used by permission from Macromedia, Inc.

Every effort has been made to trace the copyright holders.
The publisher apologizes for any unintentional omissions and would be pleased,
in such cases, to place an acknowledgment in future editions of this book.

All other images © Dorling Kindersley.
For further information see: www.dkimages.com

Microsoft® is a registered trademark of Microsoft Corporation
in the United States and/or other countries.